EVERYTHING IS OBVIOUS AFTER IT HAPPENS

poems by

Mark Gosztyla

Finishing Line Press
Georgetown, Kentucky

EVERYTHING IS OBVIOUS AFTER IT HAPPENS

Copyright © 2022 by Mark Gosztyla
ISBN 978-1-64662-841-4 First Edition
All rights reserved under International and Pan-American Copyright Conventions. No part of this book may be reproduced in any manner whatsoever without written permission from the publisher, except in the case of brief quotations embodied in critical articles and reviews.

ACKNOWLEDGMENTS

Many thanks to the editors at *Miracle Monocle* for believing in and publishing early versions of "[A ship of fools and the captain's dog], [At best, we're the best], & [Stop looking for the end, or it will never arrive]."
***
Additional thanks to my friends, teachers, & favorite lunch dates: Maria Chelko, Sarah Stickney, & Brian Wilkins; Mekeel McBride, David Rivard, & Charlie Simic; Neil Miller, Jonathan Strong, & Michael Ullman; Andy Arcand, Ellen Devine, & Stephen Siperstein.

Thank you to my family for never letting this world seem dull.

Special thanks & all my love always to Lillian, Waverly, & Amy.

Publisher: Leah Huete de Maines
Editor: Christen Kincaid
Cover Art: Annalisa Barron Studio
Author Photo: David Ottenstein
Cover Design: Elizabeth Maines McCleavy

Order online: www.finishinglinepress.com
also available on amazon.com

Author inquiries and mail orders:
Finishing Line Press
PO Box 1626
Georgetown, Kentucky 40324
USA

Contents

A ship of fools...1 The idols of a precious life...2 I walk out of the house...3 A world bathed in neon...4 Shit certain to kill...5 Little blue clouds dissolving...6 The dog that thinks...7 It's possible it's more...8 At best, we're the best...9 And after happiness...10 I said there's no future...11 Stop looking for the end...12 The path starts at the back door...13 Cereal bowls half-full of milk...14 The star ready to burst...15 A cabbie's after-dinner breath...16 Notes...17

"Reality is a cloud of possibility, not a point."
—Amos Tversky

"All the world's a stage we're going through."
—Lorrie Moore

A ship of fools and the captain's dog won't let anybody sleep with it in the lifeboat. The drop of the egg into the frying pan spitting bits of bacon grease onto the stovetop, and somehow that means everything's going to be alright. The golden run of yolk across the plate, and the tongue that wants to chase it. The mouse's tail spied underneath the coffee table like a finger of frost on the windowpane of morning like one of those people talking about America as if it could be anything other than a conspiracy theory.

The idols of a precious life now in dank basement storage. Week-old coffee grounds taken to be read by the blind woman who lives on the other side of the railroad engine's whistle. You know, where Joe used to live with his family? You've been there a hundred times. His dad builds spaceships. Or at least the stereos the astronauts listen to when they're in outer space. They spin and spin the knob, every channel hot water pouring down their body, down the body of the woman in the shower on the first day of a new job, sudden chrome silhouette on a truck, highway bound.

I walk out of the house this morning on my way to work, and the moon sticks around for a while, reflects not only a normal amount of sun but also the *I'll have some bleu cheese on that* feeling I'm feeling fat on the free lunches of yesterday. The fortune cookie that read *Never forget a friend, especially if he owes you.* After the odor of the dead thing in the bedroom wall, lilacs on a spring breeze. All the gold of first daffodils despite the bulldozing of the prior owner's garden bed, planted without the condo board's approval. All the space around these words filled with baby doll heads festooned with silver glitter. The glowing. The world of brightness.

A world bathed in neon and shimmer. Air-dried by flat skies. Sunrise like weakly brewed tea. Tug at the edge of the blanket and an early morning walk long enough to put holes in the soles of those new shell-toes. A world defined by how long it takes to cry a beard full of tears and then tear it out in clumps of fear. I know how to escape these January pants but not the socks. That's gossip. Cliché. Pop lyrics and error messages.

Shit certain to kill all who get too close. A verbal altercation over who's more vegetarian. Cosmic error of a coin with only one side. Little semi-circle of purple bruise on a fingernail from a door shut too soon. The sound of a cheap clock banging away in the kitchen all day. The drop of the faucet. All unknown qualities of personality. A door at the end of a hallway that opens only to reveal more wall. And this weather! sunny, then cloudy, then sunny again!

Little blue clouds dissolving into writing in the white of morning sky. The story of the story that turns out to be just as good as the story itself. In a language not understood but still the quickness of the heartbeat of someone who cares more than they should. Zealous tide pulling back the foamy edge of the rubber-necked baby faces that fill the college-town dive-bar turning to gape every time the door opens. Live music every Tuesday night.

The dog that thinks every plate a Frisbee. The Frisbee that thinks itself a flying saucer that thinks itself an aluminum foil pie plate filled with whipped cream to be smashed into the face of the next aghast cocktail partier exclaiming *the fact* Hitler and Trump were both *Time's Person of the Year*. Line 'em up: Gandhi, Mother-fucking-Teresa, and the Personal Computer. The dog that emerges from the sideshow and begins reciting a poem, this poem, a poem even better than this. The return of the Madison Square Garden Nazis like the gift of new towels stashed in a drafty bathroom—O luxury! O thread count!—the always delightful tingle of asshole after a liberal dusting of Goldbond!

It's possible it's more than a nap if you're lying in bed underneath the covers. The shades drawn. Daylight's slivers unlooked for. Categorize it as life at your own peril. Disregard all ground rules for discussion of future living. Some books best used as doorstops and others as a means of execution for mice stuck in kitchen countertop glue traps. Even a short-lived victory gets remembered as a W by the record books. A melting galaxy of ice cream in the bottom of the container left out on an August afternoon.

At best, we're the best. At worst, we chew cold meatballs. Drink cheap beer. Go raspberry picking in a patch full of poison ivy. Talk about desperation. Delirium. Diagram on bar napkins the ways the beginning of the end and the end are not the same thing. Both are reminders to attend to the things you can: go see a movie, cut the grass, try not to get caught by the camera picking your nose.

And after happiness is another chance for happiness. Everybody standing in the parking lot, waiting for the beer to pour, talking about other beer they've stood in line for, how long the line, yuckety-yuck. Cut to an adjacent scene between two could-have-been's, and in it one of them reads aloud from a book in their lap. The other responds by quoting some poetry from memory. It could happen. The gods of self-examination, the gods of concision, but which first? Knife handle held delicately as together, into the dark opening of the crawlspace beneath the kitchen, we peer, looking for the noise that keeps interrupting dinner. Did you say something? I thought you said something?

I said *there's no future except the one we're all making up as we go along.* You said *goodbye* like walking out of the restaurant to a parking ticket and a flat tire. The stink of the talk when there's oh-so-many people and no one's listening. All the grinning the gods are grinning found in the salt-stained cracks of the small-town sidewalks.

Stop looking for the end, or it will never arrive. Just a dialogue with the horse at the edge of the woods. You say that there's a problem. I have no problem acknowledging that that problem is me. You say it takes all the sugar we have left in the house to make the tea sweet enough to drink. My new favorite word is from the German: zugzwang, the move that gives your enemy victory. You say that's impossible because conmen all sell the same thing: themselves. When everything feels like the blah-blah-blah of an ambitious recycling project beginning.

The path starts at the back door and then bends out of sight around a field of sunflowers, labyrinth of dumb pinwheels of gold, amber, mustard, orange, cayenne. Just one question and still can't formulate the answer. Somewhere else, an altar call ends. But to continue is mostly what nobody can stop from doing. Walking like a mailman whose route is done for the day. Every day a good one to wear the underwear with hearts on them. Long-gone dream-girl on the line wanting to know why I never had the nerve to kiss her, as if taking this long to ask allowed me to sort out what I've been trying to say my whole life.

Cereal bowls half-full of milk and abandoned on bookshelves around the house. Afternoon sun low enough to fill the sky with a gold that's almost drinkable. The search between the couch cushions yields not the remote but a pair of panties. Not mine. Alas. Always the passing of the moment that makes obvious what's wrong, how to fix it, and the no-time to get anything done. Meanwhile, the season of loss that follows every win-now move continues with the usual flourishes of popcorn & discounted beers.

The star ready to burst into not-flame. The perfunctory check of Superman before entering the room full of wannabe oligarchs, morally assured despots, and the deranged determined fascist old ladies in the grocery story cereal aisle who, from the seats of their scooter-carts, don't want no help reaching their favorite brands. The difference between long-term and short-term that can feel like forever. When the necessary scarf feels like a noose on the walk home that ends the night as underfoot snowmelt refreezes. The thumbnail moon the most careful observer.

A cabbie's after-dinner breath desperate for one last fare before the end of tonight's graveyard. The clerk giving the eye to every late-night teenager paying for gas with nickels and pocket lint. Is there enough for a Big Gulp, too? The congregation of soulless candy bars always sleepily watching the patter. The way home to a fleecy-toothed morning marked by two stonewalls along a country road that floods every time it rains. Behind one, an airport filled with hopeful passengers ogling an empty tarmac. Behind the other, a patient on a gurney, abdominal cavity waiting to be sewn shut by a cheery surgeon peering in, saying to no one in particular, *One last look, to make sure we got everything we came with.*

NOTES

"Everything is obvious after it happens," is something I heard on a basketball podcast conversation between Henry Abbott and David Thorpe.

*

Amos Tversky's quote comes from Michael Lewis's book *The Undoing Project*.

*

The Lorrie Moore quote comes from her novel *Anagrams*.

Mark Gosztyla has degrees in English (BA '04) and Poetry (MFA '09) from the University of New Hampshire. His poems have appeared in *FEED, LUMINA, minnesota review, Miracle Monocle, Outlook Springs, Tinderbox Poetry Journal, & Watershed Review.* He's taught poetry & writing at The University of New Hampshire & Tufts University and is currently the Head of the English Department at Choate Rosemary Hall. He lives in Connecticut with his wife and family.

www.ingramcontent.com/pod-product-compliance
Lightning Source LLC
LaVergne TN
LVHW041525070426
835507LV00013B/1826